OLD
AYLESBURY

by

ELLIOTT VINEY, MA, FSA

and

PAMELA NIGHTINGALE, MA, PHD

White Crescent Press
LIMITED

All royalties from the
sale of this book will be given
to the St Mary's Restoration Fund.
E.V. P.N.

Printed and published by

WHITE CRESCENT PRESS LTD, LUTON

1586

Foreword
by the Lord-Lieutenant of Buckinghamshire
Major J. D. Young

I commend this book on Old Aylesbury with its many and attractive photographs. And it should be noted that all the royalties from its sale will be going to St Mary's Church Restoration Fund.

Aylesbury has for long been recognised as the capital town of Buckinghamshire, and consequently its parish church has a special status. Until the nineteenth century Buckinghamshire was simply an archdeaconry of the enormous diocese of Lincoln and because of this never has had a cathedral within its boundaries. And so if any parish church can be said to take the place of a cathedral then it must be St Mary's, and indeed whenever it is felt desirable to have a county service on important occasions then almost inevitably the choice is St Mary's, Aylesbury.

'The town properly thought of is the very crown and summit of man's creativeness and should be the vehicle for the highest manifestations of his sensibility, his love of order and seemliness, of dignity and loveliness.'

ERIC GILL – *Autobiography*, 1940

CONTENTS

Aylesbury seen from Southcourt, c. 1840; a rare engraving by N. Whittock. The building in the centre is the County Hall. On the right is the old gaol which was pulled down in 1847.

Introduction

When Queen Victoria came to the throne in 1837, the date roughly of this engraving by Whittock, the county town had a population of about 6,000 and only a few buildings separated the Market Square from the surrounding pastures on which the town's prosperity was built. In 1951 the population had reached 21,000 but when Pevsner published his *Buckinghamshire* in 1960 he could still write of Aylesbury, 'The impression is of a market town, prosperous in the eighteenth century'. Since then it has almost doubled its population, and the small market town has become an expanding centre for light industry and offices in which the atmosphere of the eighteenth century has all but disappeared. The church and County Hall which dominate the town in Whittock's engraving have been dwarfed by the concrete of the new county offices, and the whole central area from the station to the Market Square and Walton Street has been demolished and rebuilt.

The social and economic transformation of the last fifteen years has left hardly a corner of the old town untouched, and this book records what has been lost – individual buildings of dignity and grace like the Old House and Walton Cottage (Plates 60a and 61a), historic inns like the *Rising Sun* and the *Bear* (Plates 31a and 59b), and a great many more

5

seventeenth and eighteenth-century buildings, perhaps not individually of outstanding merit but giving to the town character, variety and a human scale (see, e.g. Plates 62a and 78a). With them has departed much of the spirit which gave Aylesbury its separate identity – the chapels showing its early independence in religion, as John Wilkes at the Prebendal House typified its independence in politics, fortified at the beginning of this century (for a population of 11,000) by thirty-one grocer's shops and sixty-two public houses. The intimate character of a small community was enhanced by the numerous alleys and lanes which made for familiar contacts, and by the grouping of houses which put the front doors of the more well-to-do directly on the street and cheek by jowl with their humbler neighbours (Plates 60a, 74b and 75a).

Fortunately something of this intimate character remains in what chiefly distinguishes Aylesbury, 'the intricate and interesting sequence' of its four squares, to which the planners in the 1960s, whatever else they did, happily added another. It is fascinating to watch the ebb and flow of activity from one square to another throughout the town's history. The churchyard was once noisy with grammar-school boys and the overcrowded workhouse (Plates 20b, 21a and 23b), Kingsbury with auctions (Plate 19a) and later the bus station, and the Market Square with cattle and stalls, but between-whiles there was space and quiet to stand and stare (Plate 13a).

We have arranged the photographs so that the reader can do precisely this today in an itinerary which takes him from the Market Square round the old town and Walton and back to the Market Square again.

We should like to thank the many people who have made this book possible, especially those who lent photographs. In particular we have drawn on the Osterfield Collection which is now in the County Record Office. Mr Hayward Parrott has generously put at our disposal not only many of his photographs but his invaluable knowledge of the town and saved us from several mistakes. We have also received particular help from Mr P. D. Lipson, Mr R. May and Mr W. T. Philbey.

Mr Nightingale's help has been invaluable throughout.

Elliott Viney
Pamela Nightingale

Aylesbury, Michaelmas 1976

The Market Square

7a.   A water-colour, c. 1800 by Paul Sandby, of the lower part of the Market Square showing the Tudor original Market House, demolished c. 1808. The stocks, in the centre, were last used c. 1840. A later view of the houses on the left is in Plate 13b.

7b.   An engraving of the Market Square, c. 1850, looking towards Market Street with the 'George' Hotel and the Old Bank (now Lloyd's) on the right. Founded by William Rickford and his father in 1795, it is the oldest surviving bank in the town. The 'George' Hotel was replaced by Burton's in 1936; the George Bodega still stands (cf. Plate 15a).

8a. *A horse fair, c. 1910, showing the County Hall which was completed in 1740. Originally there was a balcony outside the central window (the 'new drop') from which felons were publicly hanged.*

8b. *The court of c. 1740 in the County Hall before it was burnt in 1970. The original oak came from Wing Park. There is a cupboard in the recess behind the judge's seat for his chamber-pot – and in the eighteenth century that recess was thought private enough! The room has been faithfully rebuilt – down to the chamber-pot bearing the Hanoverian arms.*

9a.   Next to the County Hall, the 'Bell' Hotel – decorated for the coronation in 1902. The front was altered in 1919.

9b.   This triumphal arch, celebrating the same occasion, spanned the top of Walton Street. Mr Slade, the town crier, is in the foreground. Note the sign 'Money Lent' on Lucas's, the furniture shop, then also a pawnbroker's.

10a.   The 'White Hart', which was built in 1814 on the other side of the County Hall, was pulled down in 1864 to make way for the Corn Exchange. It had extensive gardens and a bowling green, and replaced a fifteenth-century inn of the same name. The figure is on the modern 'White Hart' in Exchange Street.

10b.   The Market Square, c. 1910, looking towards the County Hall and Town-Hall arches. The clock-tower was built in 1876–77. Cattle were sold in the Market Square until 1927.

11a. The Market Square, c. 1860, with the 'Green Man' Inn on the right. The later Market House, which was demolished in 1866, is seen with its adjacent shops in front of the 'George' Hotel. The office of the Bucks Herald is next to the 'Green Man'.

11b. The Market Square, in the mid-1920s showing the 'Bull's Head' Hotel in Hale-Leys Square, with Hale-Leys Passage which still exists visible on the right of the hotel.

12a.   We know that there was a 'Bull's Head' in the fifteenth century, but it was largely rebuilt to this design in the eighteenth century.

12b.   In the 1920s a false timbered front was added by its proprietor, G. Gargini, later mayor (v. Plate 92a). It was demolished in 1969.

13a. The Market Square, looking towards the 'George', after the Market House was pulled down in 1866 and before the clock-tower was put up ten years later.

13b. The south-east corner of the Market Square showing the junction with Great Western Street c. 1960. All these buildings were demolished in 1962–63 to make way for the new shopping centre. Next to the 'Coach & Horses' is the 'Cross Keys'.

14a.   The fifteenth-century 'King's Head' in 1962 after the demolition of the buildings in front of it which have since been replaced by a modern block. It has one of the few surviving inn yards in Aylesbury, and its hall is a fine example of medieval domestic architecture, with some fifteenth and sixteenth-century glass in its windows.

14b.   The corner of the Market Square and Market Street showing the entrance to the 'King's Head', c. 1910.

15a.   The Market Square, showing the War Memorial, c. 1920, with the 'George' Hotel on the right and Field's shop, which largely survives, next to the entrance to the 'King's Head'. The Fields were from 1804 until after the First World War important clockmakers and jewellers in the town; they took over the eighteenth-century business of the Quartermaines, and their shop, dated 1765, originally housed the Old Bank.

15b.   The junction of the Market Square, the High Street, Cambridge Street, Buckingham Street and Kingsbury, c. 1914, showing the statue of John Hampden (1911), the Round House, which was later rebuilt, and the sixteenth-century building which was replaced by Brook House in the 1930s.

16a.   The same spot in an engraving by J. D. Cooper from Alfred Rimmer's Ancient Streets & Homesteads of England, *published in 1879. It shows at the entrance to Kingsbury the sixteenth-century 'Black Swan' which was pulled down in 1883.*

16b.   A similar view, probably Edwardian. The water-cart loading on the right was used to lay the dust on the roads.

17a. Kingsbury in 1897. The Victorian building in the centre was then an engineer's and later bore the words 'Aeroplanes Repaired' on the roof; it was replaced 1972–73. On its left was Samuels's printing works. Notice the 'Angel's elaborate bracket arm.

17b. Kingsbury, c. 1922, showing the early seventeenth-century 'Rockwood' Inn with its timber framing exposed. The 'Red Lion' on the left was built c. 1600. Its yard, which was entered by the main doors in the centre, has recently been built over. Between the 'Red Lion' and the 'Rockwood' there was still a front garden or two. The drinking fountain stood there from 1914 till 1929 and is now in the Vale public park.

18a.   Kingsbury, c. 1890, with the 'Red Lion' on the right and beyond it the 'Angel' Inn which was demolished in the 1920s. The pump in the right foreground stood there from 1838 to 1894. On the left, with the hanging sign, is the 'Eagle', a seventeenth-century building which was a public house until 1975.

18b.   'Lifeboat Saturday' in Kingsbury at the turn of the century. The boy leaning out of the window on the left is Charles Ivatts, the last of seven generations of the family which founded Ivatts' shoe business in 1723.

19a.   Kingsbury in the 1920s, showing the English tank which was displayed there from 1920. When being broken up before the construction of the bus station in June 1929 the tank blew up. The goods displayed are about to be sold by the Aylesbury auctioneer, Mr Millburn.

19b.   Pebble Lane, formerly Church Row, in 1947 showing the seventeenth-century 'Foresters' Arms' and a corner of the 'Rockwood'. This is one of the few streets in Aylesbury which has kept the medieval feature of a kennel or central drain. The Victoria Working Men's Club, which was built in 1887, is on the right.

20a.   Pebble Lane, with the pump on the left which was installed in the 1840s. It was placed at that height to fill the water-carts. The church parapet is being pulled down after it was damaged in the great gale of 2 January 1976. The building out of sight behind the low wall on the right was originally the British School, which was rebuilt in 1873 and has since served the town as library and clinic.

St Mary's Square

20b.   St Mary's Square, showing the parish halls on the right. Beyond are the seventeenth-century houses which until 1829 served as the parish workhouse or poorhouse. Some of the poor made lace and baked bread; the ovens survive in the cellars. On the left can just be seen the caretaker's house of the chapel built in 1878 by the Bucks Evangelistic Mission which was replaced by the present Evangelical Church in the 1960s.

21a. An engraving by N. Whittock of St Mary's Church, c. 1840, before Gilbert Scott's restoration of 1848–69 which substituted three lancet windows for the fifteenth-century east window. The remains of this window have been rebuilt in the garden of Green End House. The prominent south porch was demolished at the same time. The Grammar School then occupied what is now the Museum, but the top form worked in the south chapel; this print shows some of the boys on the left.

21b. Flint Cottage in Granville Place, which runs off Granville Street. A brick-and-flint cottage, ornamented with bottle-ends, which was built in 1854 and is one of the few houses to survive in this street.

22a.   St Mary's Square, showing the 'Derby Arms' which was built as a private house in the seventeenth century. Its handsome tall front is early Georgian.

22b.   A water-colour, c. 1910, of the 'Barley Mow' at the top of Nelson Terrace. It was built in the eighteenth century and is now a private house.

23a. *The west side of St Mary's Square, c. 1950, with eighteenth-century cottages on the right and the only iron railings to survive the war.*

23b. *St Mary's Square, c. 1900, showing the Museum, built in 1719 as the Grammar School. To the left is the late eighteenth-century Latin School, now one of the parish halls, to the right of which a replica was built in 1907. Note the railings round the churchyard and the tombs.*

24a.   Early seventeenth-century cottages in Parsons Fee used as a school c. 1800, and the corner of Hickman's Almshouses. Thomas Hickman's bequest was made in 1695 but the 'five large cottages by the church gate' were rebuilt in 1871 and reconstructed internally in 1975. Notice the detail of No 5's timber framing.

24b.   The Prebendal House seen from the churchyard; so called because for centuries the church manor belonged to the diocese of Lincoln. The eighteenth-century house was from 1749 to 1764 the home of John Wilkes, the radical politician who was MP for Aylesbury from 1757 until he was forced into exile in 1764. On this part of the churchyard wall is the tablet which Wilkes put up to his gardener, John Smart.

Church Street and Temple Street

25a. *Church Street in the 1890s showing the Grammar School on the right, and on the left, No 12, an early seventeenth-century gabled cottage with Georgian shop windows. On the immediate left is The Chantry, a sixteenth-century house to which a gothick front was added c. 1840.*

25b. *Church Street before the 1920s showing the fine porch of Ceely House which was acquired by the Museum in 1946. The buildings on the left are as they were before Lincoln House was built in the 1960s.*

26a.   The Stables of Ceely House in 1912 when it was a doctor's house and surgery. Miss
Cicely Baker, whose home it was, is holding the pony's bridle. Church Street was mainly
where doctors used to live and practise. The last was Dr Gimson at The Chantry (see Plate
25a) who retired in 1975.

26b.   Temple Square at the turn of the century. The shop on the right was owned by
R. Thorp, the bacon factor. Its front has since been extended to the left.

27a.   Temple Square at the same date, showing the seventeenth-century 'Queen's Head' and a military parade.

27b.   Temple Street, c. 1910, showing Theobald's china shop. The street was originally Cordwainers Street or Cobblers Row, and was renamed in the eighteenth century after the Temple family of Stowe.

28a.   Temple Street, c. 1910. The buildings on the left are mostly eighteenth-century. Many of the shop-fronts have been altered as the shops of grocers, fruiterers, fishmongers, butchers and bootmakers have given way to estate agents' offices.

28b.   Temple Square, looking down Castle Street, c. 1910. The buildings on the right have since been restored to be more in keeping with their original eighteenth-century design. The late Georgian house on the left was at this time the offices of the Inland Revenue Commissioners, but was formerly a school, and more recently was Dr Taylor's house and surgery.

Castle Street

29a. Castle Street in the 1890s. The fine down-pipe of what was then the 'Black Horse' bears the date 1722; the bracket of the inn-sign remains. The tall building on the left was built as an Independent Chapel in 1788. It was later a lecture hall and then a Labour club. Gravestones of nonconformists up to c. 1883 are in the garden behind.

29b. Looking up Castle Street towards Temple Square, c. 1950. The house on the right, No 23, is mid-sixteenth-century and has since had its timber framing exposed. Note its eighteenth-century double steps.

29

30a. St Osyth's in Parsons Fee, the former Prebendal (i.e. church) farmhouse. The lowest building of the group is c. 1650, the middle is probably late Tudor, and the main house was built in the late seventeenth century. Since this photograph was taken in 1947 the windows of the middle block have been altered.

30b. The Prebendal tithe-barn seen from the Prebendal kitchen gardens. It was built in the late sixteenth century to store the church's tax in kind of one-tenth of all agricultural produce. It is now used as a workshop.

31a. *The seventeenth-century 'Rising Sun' at the junction of Castle Street (on the left) and the old Oxford Road opposite St Mary's School. It was demolished in 1963 to make way for the inner ring road. Edward Cook (with the crutch) worked as a cobbler in the 1930s in the workshop attached to 10 St Mary's Square (see Plate 22 right).*

31b. *The old Oxford Road c. 1885 at its junction with Castle Street, showing the 'Rising Sun' on the extreme right. The cottages along the Oxford Road have been demolished but some of the houses at the bottom of Castle Street survive. The field in the foreground is now the playground of St Mary's School which was built in 1850.*

White Hill

32a.   The original 'Hen and Chickens' at the junction of White Hill and the old Oxford Road in 1965. It was pulled down to make way for the ring road and a second public house of the same name was built in the corner of the Prebendal gardens.

32b.   Looking down White Hill c. 1910 to the site of the present roundabout at the junction of the Oxford and Friarage Roads.

33a.   Looking up White Hill c. 1910 from the site of the same roundabout with the Prebendal wall and gardens on the right. Many of the cottagers in this area kept ducks and it was originally known as the Common Dunghill.

33b.   The same view taken from lower down. On the left is the 'Seven Stars' public house. The 'Hen and Chickens' was to the right of the picture.

34a. Seventeenth-century cottages in Whitehall Row which led off White Hill opposite Ripon Street. They were demolished in the 1920s. There were said to be twenty-one alleys in this area in which some 700 people lived in 158 cottages.

34b. Similar cottages in Whitehall Court which ran parallel with Whitehall Row, 1925.

35a. Whitehall Street showing the entrance to Ripon Street, on 26 April 1908.

35b. The Royal Bucks Hospital in 1899. It was originally converted from a country house in 1833, but it was rebuilt under the guidance of Florence Nightingale acting through her brother-in-law, Sir Harry Verney, in 1859–60. A further floor was added to the right-hand part of the building in the 1930s.

36a.   The junction of the Bicester Road and Whitehall Street at the Royal Bucks round-about c. 1960 showing the 'Plough' Inn, soon to be demolished for the ring road. The building on the left was the Aylesbury Motor Company which was demolished with the neighbouring sixteenth-century house to make way for Pond's garage.

36b.   Ardenham House, opposite the Royal Bucks, an elegant house built 1780–90 by the sister-in-law of the sculptor Nollekens who is thought to have influenced its design. The gate-way has been demolished and the rendering removed.

The Bicester Road

37a.   The Bicester Road c. 1900, looking up towards the Royal Bucks. The houses were a late nineteenth-century development.

37b.   The Bicester Road c. 1900. The site of Keith Garages is on the left. The gallows were on the corner of Griffin Lane before they were re-erected at the County Hall; hence the original name of Gallows Road.

38a.   Dunsham Lane in the 1960s before the building of the Elmhurst estate. The lane was a track from the Buckingham Road to Dunsham farm.

Buckingham Street

38b.   Putnam House, a pair of town houses built in the 1840s in Buckingham Street next to the present sub post office. They were demolished in 1970.

39a. Buckingham Street, looking towards the town centre, before the building of the Methodist Church in 1893. The entrance to Granville Street is on the right.

39b. Buckingham Street c. 1910 showing the Methodist Church. The shops to the right of it were demolished in the early 1960s to make way for an office block. The building with the balcony was Jenns', the furnisher's. The house to the right of the chapel was the office of the Rural District Council until c. 1962.

40a.   The corner of Buckingham Street and Kingsbury c. 1890. The shops in the centre were recently demolished but the timber-framing of the adjoining building on the left can still be seen. Note the cottages in the background in Kingsbury on the site of a modern office block.

40b.   Back Buckingham Street, c. 1890. The 'Two Brewers' on the left survives and the seventeenth-century buildings on the right mostly remain but with altered fronts.

41a. Back Buckingham Street from its junction with Cambridge Street, c. 1908, showing the 'Harrow' Inn, the main structure of which probably dates from the seventeenth century.

Cambridge Street

41b. Looking down Cambridge Street from near Kingsbury c. 1860, showing the seventeenth-century 'Barleycorn' (left) and a row of eighteenth-century houses (right).

42a.   The same view in 1907 showing Millburn's auction room, the tall building with a bay window on the right.

42b.   Bakers-Lane Chapel, the first Baptist meeting-place in the town, built in 1733 in Bakers Lane, now Cambridge Street, on a site behind the row of shops next to the Odeon cinema. It was subsequently occupied by other denominations, including the Plymouth Brethren, and was demolished in 1938.

43a. St John's Church, Cambridge Street, opened in 1883 as a daughter church of St Mary's and demolished in 1970. The site was bought by the Post Office for an extension of the telephone exchange and its car-park.

43b. St John's School shown after the church's demolition and just before its own two years later. It was built in 1856. The corner of the telephone exchange is on the left.

44a. Seventeenth-century timber-framed cottages in Nag's-Head Court off Cambridge Street, now the site of the Upper-Hundreds car-park.

The High Street

Formerly known as New Road, the High Street was completed in 1826 to shorten the route into the town centre from the Tring Road which previously came into the Wendover Road near the 'Broad Leys' Inn.

44b. The High Street seen from the Market Square, c. 1910, showing the 'Crown' Hotel which was much altered and reduced in size when the New Road was built. The building seen here was demolished in 1937 and replaced by shops and offices. Disraeli's statue now stands in the corner on the right.

45a. The High Street, c. 1920, looking into the Market Square. On the right is the Union of London & Smith's Bank which was rebuilt in 1976 as the National Westminster. Beyond it are the original shops which are still occupied by W. Thrasher and V. H. Jarvis. Opposite them is the 'Crown' Hotel.

45b. Looking up the High Street in 1860 towards the Union of London & Smith's Bank. At this time there were private houses on both sides of the street.

46a. Looking up the High Street from the Post Office in 1908 showing Longley's, the large draper's shop which was demolished in 1938 to make way for Marks & Spencer's.

46b. Hale-Leys Chapel, founded in 1707 for the Presbyterians but altered and enlarged in 1818 after it had become an Independent Chapel. It was entirely rebuilt in 1874 as a Congregational Church. The Hale Leys was the name of the meadowland which served as the town's recreation ground before the New Road was made.

47a.   Looking down the High Street from Britannia Street, c. 1890, showing a Sunday procession. The houses on the left with their front areas have been replaced by shops. Those on the opposite side remain but shop-fronts now project from them on the ground floor.

47b.   The first St Joseph's Catholic Church, an iron building of 1892 demolished in 1935 when it was replaced by the present building.

48a.   The town's first railway station, c. 1860 with the 'George' Hotel's cab standing outside. It was built in 1839 at the corner of Railway Street and Station Street when the railway opened as a single-track branch line from Cheddington on the London and Birmingham main line. It was replaced by the new station (below).

48b.   The High Street in 1915 showing the 2nd Bucks Battalion marching past the London & North-Western railway station which was built on this site in 1889. It was closed to passenger traffic in 1953 and pulled down in 1960. This line closed completely with the ending of freight traffic on 2 December 1963. The milk float was driven by W. Cartwright, whose family still run the Buckingham-Street dairy.

49a. *Looking up the High Street in the 1920s before the Vale Park was made to the right of the photograph. The buildings on the left are mostly unchanged. Note the dirt on the surface of the street – still a common sight at the time.*

49b. *The High Street looking down to Hazell's Corner from the canal bridge in 1902. On the left is the distinctive wall and clock of Nestlé's condensed-milk factory built for the Aylesbury Condensed-Milk company in 1870.*

50a.   *This part of Park Street was once called Mill Terrace after Hills & Partridge's flour mill. When these three Baldwin children were photographed here c. 1896 the terrace was often flooded for more than a week at a time by the canal and the Bear Brook.*

50b.   *The railway line to Cheddington north–east of the level crossing in Park Street, c. 1910. The Stocklake houses on the right are unchanged. On the left are the grounds of the Manor House on Bierton Hill.*

Bierton Hill

51a. The new County Gaol built on Bierton Hill in 1847. It was designed by Major Jebb of the Royal Engineers with the intention that prisoners should not be able to communicate with each other. The two houses on either side of the gateway were for the governor and the chaplain. The last public hanging took place here in the 1860s.

51b. The Aylesbury Union workhouse built in 1844 to replace the original parish workhouse in St Mary's Square and the intervening one in the Oxford Road which was built in 1829 on the site of what is now Mount Street and St Mary's School. The workhouse became the Tindal Hospital in the last war when wards were added at the back to accommodate the Middlesex Hospital which had been evacuated from London.

The Tring Road

52a.   The Tring Road showing the printing works of Hazell, Watson & Viney in 1913. The firm, which has been the largest employer in the town for nearly a century, was founded in London in 1839, opened a branch at Aylesbury at California (just south of the station) in 1867 and moved to this site eleven years later.

52b.   The first houses in Walton Way built by Hazell's for their employees in 1920. At the time these were the last houses in the Tring Road.

53a.   The Grammar School, soon after it was built on its present site in 1906, after moving from its original home which is now the County Museum.

53b.   Turnfurlong, where it leaves Walton Road, c. 1920.

WALTON GRANGE

54a.   *Walton Grange. A drawing of the sixteenth-century brick and timber L-shaped house on the site of the present Girls' High School. For many years it was the home of the Hazell family until it was demolished after being severely damaged by a landmine which fell by Walton Pond in the Second World War. This was the only bomb to fall on Aylesbury during the war.*

54b.   *Walton Road, c. 1900, showing the barn of Walton Grange on the right. On the left is a seventeenth-century weather-boarded house and barn which were converted into a malting-house in the eighteenth century; part of the barn still remains. The seventeenth-century cottages in the left foreground with falling shutters have been demolished.*

55a.   Walton Pond, c. 1900, showing cottages which were demolished by the landmine. An old people's home now stands to the right of the picture. Note the large number of ducks.

55b.   The junction of the Wendover and Walton Roads, c. 1860. The house on the left survives although the Midland Bank has been built to the left of it. A hundred yards down the Wendover Road can be seen the old toll-gate and toll-house which were demolished in 1878; round the corner another gate barred the Stoke Road and the toll-house for this remains. The house on the right survives as a shop.

56a. A late-Victorian view of Walton Terrace, a row of mainly Regency houses, with Holy-Trinity Church, which was built in 1845, in the distance. On the other side of the road was land belonging to Walton-Court farm.

56b. The Holy-Trinity side of Walton Street, nearer to Aylesbury, shortly before the demolition of most of these buildings to make way for offices in the 1960s.

57a.   Looking down Walton Street towards the town centre, c. 1918. The first houses on the right with the church school were replaced by Holy-Trinity church-hall in 1927.

57b.   Walton Street looking towards Wendover in the 1950s. Demolition of the south side had already started. On the left can be seen part of the large premises of the Aylesbury Brewery Company on the site now occupied by Planair House. The spire of Holy-Trinity Church is in the background.

58a.   *Walton-Street Baptist Chapel, c. 1900. It was built in 1828 and altered in 1895 when the tracery was inserted in the windows and the pediment over the door was embellished. Probably the lower windows were added at the same time. It was demolished in 1966, and the site (on the railway side of Walton Street opposite the canal basin) is now occupied by a garage. The house next door belonged to F. E. Fisher, the cab-owner.*

58b.   *The interior of the boatmen's chapel at the canal basin, c. 1920.*

59a.   The canal basin seen from Walton Street in 1966. The Aylesbury branch of the Grand Junction Canal was opened in 1814 to bring coals from the Midlands. It reduced the price from 2s 6d to 1s 3d a cwt.

59b.   The seventeenth-century 'Bear' Inn photographed in 1964 shortly before its demolition. The site is now occupied by the offices of solicitors next to those of the Bucks Herald.

60a.   *The Old House photographed in 1966 shortly before its demolition to make way for the Walton-Street roundabout. It was built in the eighteenth century by Acton Chaplin, Clerk of the Peace and Treasurer of the County. In 1799 he employed prisoners from the gaol nearby to lay out the extensive gardens and the lake which still exists beyond the ring road. The porch has been re-erected at the Old Rectory, Pitchcott.*

60b.   *Exchange Street at its junction with Walton Street, in 1935. The houses on the left were demolished that year to make way for the Police Station and the County Constabulary's Headquarters. Cogger & Hawkins' garage can be seen on the right with the cattle market on the left, and the chestnuts of the Recreation Ground beyond.*

61a. *Walton Cottage in 1947. An early Regency house occupying the present site of the County Library next to the Old House; it was demolished in 1963. The garden of this house extended as far as the railway and included the site of the multi-storey car-park.*

61b. *The 'White Swan' side of Walton Street before the building of the first County Council offices in 1929. The large house in the centre of the photograph was the official residence of the County's chief constable. The house at the far end, beyond the lamp-post, still remains.*

62a. The top of Walton Street in 1903 showing on the left the seventeenth-century 'White Swan' and the chief constable's house, and on the right the buildings which stood on the present site of Woolworth's. These included the premises of J. K. H. Fowler, the wine-and-spirit merchant, and next to Walton Cottage before 1939 there was a working smithy (see Plate 82b).

62b. The corner of Walton and Great Western Streets in 1964, now the site of Woolworth's. The new County offices can be seen under construction on the left.

Great Western Street

63a. Great Western Street looking towards the 'Bell' in the Market Square, c. 1960. The 'Falcon' on the left and the 'Greyhound' in the centre were demolished in the early 1960s. The name and licence of the 'Greyhound' were transferred to a new public house in Churchill Avenue.

63b. The old Friarage Road looking towards Great Western Street in 1964. The seventeenth-century buildings on the left were part of a slaughter-house.

64a   The 'Railway Hotel' in Great Western Street, built in 1898 and demolished in 1966 for the ring road. It was described by Pevsner as 'an engaging little horror'. One of the gargoyles on the roof is now in the County Museum.

64b.   The Bucks Herald's *printing works by the station yard, demolished in 1966 for the access road to the multi-storey car-park.*

Silver Street

65a. *An eighteenth-century print showing the top of Walton Street with the 'White Swan' on the right, the entrance to Great Western Street on the left, and looking up into Silver Street.*

65b. *Silver Street, c. 1960, a street of mainly sixteenth and seventeenth-century houses with later fronts. The 'Dark Lantern' is the white building at the top of the street on the right. The street was demolished, apart from the 'Dark Lantern' and Jones & Cocks's, to make way for the new shopping centre.*

66a.   The north side of Silver Street in 1964 shortly before its demolition, showing the 'Dark Lantern' and Jones & Cocks's shop at the top of the street.

66b.   Looking down Silver Street, c. 1910, towards Walton Street. The public house in the foreground was the 'White Horse' which fronted on the Market Square. It ceased to be a pub between the wars and became the 'Old Beams' restaurant (see Plate 68b).

67a. The back of the houses in Silver Street illustrated in Plate 65b showing their timber framing. The photograph was taken in 1964 from the site of the present pedestrian crossing in Great Western Street.

67b. Silver Lane, which ran parallel with Bourbon Street from the old Friarage Road across the top of Silver Street to the Market Square; the passage through to the square next to Jones & Cocks still exists. On the left of the picture were originally nine cottages which were demolished before 1964 when this photograph was taken.

68a. The 'Dark Lantern', c. 1960. The building dates from the sixteenth century and was surrounded by narrow alleys. After the demolition of the surrounding buildings in the 1960s the outside was considerably altered.

68b. One of the passages, now blocked up, which ran from Silver Lane into the Market Square. This one ran under the 'Old Beams' restaurant, formerly the 'White Horse' (see Plate 66b).

Bourbon Street

(see also Page 76)

69a. Looking down Temple Street to the corner of Market Street and Bourbon Street in the early 1960s before the demolition of the well-known Aylesbury grocer's, M. T. Cocks.

69b. Bourbon Street and Market Street seen from the 'Queen Victoria', c. 1960, before the demolition of all the buildings on the right of Bourbon Street which made way for the new shopping centre.

70a.   Looking from the top of Rickfords Hill, with The Friarage on the right to Dell's brewery. The Dells (see Plate 94a) were a leading Aylesbury family for many generations and lived in Bedford House, now Barclay's Bank, in the Market Square. The brewery was demolished to make way for the public baths.

70b.   The public baths at the junction of the old Friarage Road and Bourbon Street. They were opened in 1895 as 'Public Swimming and Private Slipper Baths' and they were demolished in 1960.

71a.   The Methodist Chapel in Friarage Passage, built in 1837. It was later used as the Comrades (Ex-Services) Club until demolished to make way for the shopping centre.

71b.   Friarage Passage, originally called Friars' Path, which ran through the site of the fourteenth-century friary. The stones still to be seen at the base of the brick wall at the top of the passage may well be part of the original wall of the friary. The bridge in the photograph still exists crossing the Bear Brook to the station. The garden of The Friarage ran down to the brook before the construction of the ring road.

72a.   The station yard, c. 1960, looking up Great Western Street before the building of the new Friarage Road. The Bucks Motor Company occupied the large garage in the left background, formerly Seaton's stables. Seaton was the proprietor of the 'George' Hotel and supplied horses for the town's fire brigade. The town's present railway station was first built in 1863 when a branch of the Great Western Railway was constructed from Princes Risborough. In 1868 the line was extended north to Verney Junction and in 1891 the Metropolitan Line from Baker Street was completed to Aylesbury.

72b.   The 4.38 pm from Marylebone about to leave Aylesbury on the last day of through working to Nottingham, 3 September 1966. After this day there were no more steam passenger trains in Aylesbury. The new County Council offices had just been completed and work was about to begin on the multi-storey car-park.

73a.   *Friarscroft, built before the First World War by William Crouch, Clerk of the Peace, at the bottom of Rickfords Hill where it joined the Oxford Road, now the double-track Friarage Road. Houses in Great Western Street can be seen in the background.*

73b.   *The 'Wheatsheaf' public house in the Oxford Road, now Friarage Road, near the junction with Rickfords Hill. The building, with neighbouring cottages, was pulled down in the early 1960s to make way for the ring road.*

74a.   Green End House on Rickfords Hill in 1865. The front is an early nineteenth-century refacing of a seventeenth-century brick house which in its turn incorporates a Tudor wing. The street was formerly Pitches Hill but was renamed after William Rickford who lived in this house from 1795 till 1855. He founded the Old Bank, now Lloyd's in the Market Square, was a leading figure in the town and its MP from 1818 till 1841.

74b.   Early eighteenth-century cottages next to Green End House, photographed c. 1900 showing the entrance to Thorp's bacon factory. Reuben Dorrell and his pony are in the foreground.

75a. *Seventeenth and eighteenth-century cottages on Rickfords Hill opposite The Friarage with the brewery in the background, photographed before 1895. Part of the 'Saracen's Head' can be seen on the left with its original brick front. Next to it is the entrance to the Quakers' meeting house and beyond are two cottages which have been completely refronted.*

75b. *The 'Saracen's Head', dating from the late seventeenth century, photographed in 1947 just before its front was altered.*

76a.   Bourbon Street in 1965 after the demolition of the south side of the street. Most of the buildings date from the mid eighteenth century. Originally Waterhouse Street, it was renamed to commemorate the residence of the French royal family at Hartwell House during the Napoleonic wars. The offices on the left are those of Parrott & Coales who have been solicitors in the town since 1775.

76b.   The corner of Bourbon Street and Temple Street just before the demolition of the corner building in 1974. Behind the nineteenth-century front was a timber-framed building. Archaeological work on the site discovered the line of the late-Saxon town ditch running along Bourbon Street and showed the probable extent of the fortified town.

77a. The confectionery shop, part of a sixteenth-century building, at the corner of Market Street and Silver Street which was demolished in the 1960s to make way for a modern block.

77b. The same building, c. 1900, showing its three-gabled front to Market Street with M. T. Cocks's grocer's shop in the background. Dukes' china business was in Aylesbury before 1812.

78a.   The other side of Market Street, c. 1918, showing the seventeenth-century buildings with eighteenth-century fronts which were in front of the 'King's Head' (see Page 14).

78b.   A view of the same buildings taken shortly before they were demolished in 1962 and New Oxford House was put in their place.

Aerial Views

79a. The Rivet works photographed from the air in 1921 showing Chiltern Street on the left. Beyond the railway line can be seen Walton Nurseries and the farm from which the Hodgkins family supplied much of Aylesbury's milk. Houses on the Wendover Road can be seen on the right.

The next three views were taken in 1966 from the scaffolding of the new County Offices looking over the west and north parts of the town.

79b. The houses to the left in Great Western Street were on the site of what is now the station roundabout in the new Friarage Road. Part of the northbound carriageway has just been laid, and can be seen cutting through the gardens of The Friarage and Friarscroft which ran right down to the Bear Brook.

80a. In the centre of this view the old Friarage Road can be seen climbing from Great Western Street to its junction with Bourbon Street. By this time several buildings, like the public baths, have been demolished and their sites used as temporary car-parks. Everything in the foreground was soon to go.

80b. The large building in the foreground with the skylights was Lucas's furniture shop and is now the site of Woolworth's. Silver Street can be seen running up towards the left, and stalls are in the Market Square. The tall part of the County Hall, plainly visible on the right, is the Crown Court.

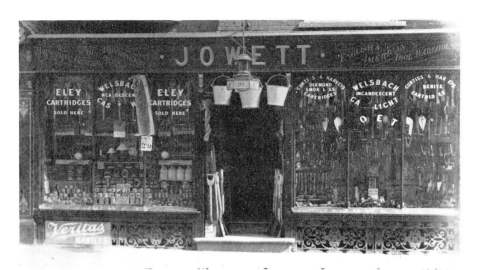

81a. Jowett's shop in Kingsbury in 1895. Notice the decorative ironwork beneath the windows which was removed in 1923 when the present windows were put in.

81b. The interior of the Misses Grinnell's tannery shop, 15 Temple Street. It was closed in 1922 and the interior remained untouched until this photograph was taken in 1940.

82a.   *Across the street was the shop of A. E. Felix, bootmaker, photographed in 1947. It demonstrates the surviving connection, which had begun in the middle ages, between Temple Street – formerly Cobblers Row – and the leather trades. The house is now an estate agent's office, but the fine eighteenth-century door and shop-window are unaltered.*

82b.   *The blacksmiths, Fred Philbey and John Brigginshaw, who worked for Mr Harry Lepper in the Walton-Street smithy (see Plates 62a and 93b).*

83a. The butcher's shop near the corner of Upper Hundreds and Cambridge Street, now Mr Lipson's antique shop.

83b. George Brown, the fishmonger, at his stall in the Market Square c. 1950; he was the son of Freddie Brown (Plate 84b).

84a.   Brown's the poulterers, in Cambridge Street, decorated for Christmas c. 1900.

84b.   Freddie Brown, costermonger of Maldon Terrace, c. 1920.

84

85a. Women Monotype keyboard operators at Hazell's in 1911.

85b. Hazell's fire brigade at the old main entrance to the printing works in the 1880s.

Groups

86a.   St Mary's church choir in 1861 photographed in the Prebendal gardens in front of the west door of the church.

86b.   St John's schoolchildren, c. 1890.

87a.   Hazell's band photographed in the 1880s before they acquired uniforms.

87b.   Special constables enlisted at the Rivet works during the General Strike of May 1926. Note the reference to Iris cars which were made at the works.

Historic Occasions

88a. *Princess Victoria, daughter of King Edward VII, visits the Royal Bucks Hospital in 1906.*

88b. *The visit of the Duke of York, later King George VI, to Aylesbury in 1928. The Mayor was Viscount Stopford.*

89a. Field Marshal Lord Roberts (wearing the cocked hat in the foreground) in the Market Square in 1910 when he unveiled the statue of Lord Chesham. The Royal Bucks Hussars formed the guard-of-honour. The photographer was Mr Millburn.

89b. 'B' Company of the Bucks Battalion fire a 'feu-de-joie' on 5 May 1935 at the local celebration of King George V's silver jubilee. This was just before the demolition of the 'George' Hotel in the background.

90a. *Aylesbury's first mayor (1917–19), Alderman R. W. Locke, inspecting the town's fire brigade, c. 1917. With him is the Lord-Lieutenant of the County, the Marquess of Lincolnshire.*

90b. *Mr Justice Edmund Davies (left) and Mr Justice Glyn-Jones leave St Mary's Church on 7 April 1964 after the Assize Service shortly before sentences were passed at the conclusion of the Great Train Robbery trial at the Aylesbury Assizes. The High Sheriff of Bucks, Elliott Viney, leads the procession and the escort of policemen carrying pikes lines the path. The Michaelmas Assize of 1970 was the last in Aylesbury.*

91a. Four honorary freemen of the Borough of Aylesbury, (left to right) Sir Ludwig Guttman, founder of the spinal unit at Stoke Mandeville hospital; the Countess of Courtown; Mrs Olive Paterson, Mayor 1939–45; Mr Harold Crookes, Town Clerk 1925–56.

91b. Lifeboat Day, c. 1951 and (left to right) Charles Ivatts, last of the boot-and-shoe dynasty of Kingsbury; Harold Watsham; Mrs Kate White, Mayor 1951–53.

92a.   Giacomo Gargini, proprietor of the 'Bull's Head' Hotel between the wars, and Mayor 1932–35.

92b.   Mr William ('Pigeon') Green photographed in 1950 with the carnation he always wore. For years he gathered manure from the streets, beat carpets, and carried sand from the Hartwell sandpits for 3d and 6d a load.

93a. Jimmy Goodwin, another well-known Aylesbury character, c. 1910.

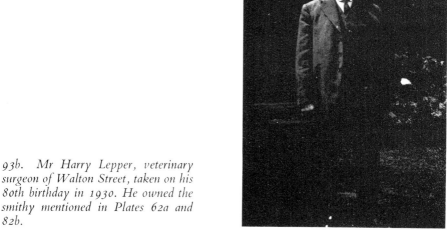

93b. Mr Harry Lepper, veterinary surgeon of Walton Street, taken on his 80th birthday in 1930. He owned the smithy mentioned in Plates 62a and 82b.

94a. A very early photograph taken in the 1850s of Mr Thomas Dell, brewer and churchwarden, with his telescope at Walton House.

Sports

94b. Aylesbury racecourse in 1906 on the fields now occupied by the Southcourt housing estate. The grandstand was approximately on the site of the present 'Greyhound' public house. The racecourse was moved to the Tring Road in 1926.

95a. The first meet of the Aylesbury and District Automobile Club in 1904. The number plate of the car on the left shows it was the 36th to be licensed in the county; the driver was Dr T. G. Parrott.

95b. The Whaddon-Chase hounds arriving for a meet in the Market Square in the early 1920s.

ACKNOWLEDGEMENTS

C. Adams, Esq: 12b, 21a, 46a, 53a, 78a, 78b.

Miss C. Baker: 26a.

Bucks Advertiser: 79b, 80a, 80b, 92b, 95b.

Aylesbury Vale District Council: 13b, 23a, 36a, 57b, 63a, 65b, 70a, 72a, 91a, 92a.

J. T. Baldwin, Esq: 50a.

Bucks County Museum: 16a, 18a, 29a, 36b, 45b, 47b, 76b, 81b.

Bucks County Record Office: Cover, 17b.

Maurice Cousins Photography: 20a, 21b.

E. Kent, Esq: 15b, 42a.

C. Lamb, Esq: 31b.

P. D. Lipson, Esq: 11a, 11b, 27b, 28a, 45a, 47a, 49b, 52a, 62a, 66b, 83a, 88a, 94b, 100.

P. Locke, Esq: 90a.

R. May, Esq: 9b, 14b, 28b, 37a, 40a, 41a, 49a, 77a, 89a.

J. R. Millburn, Esq: 19a, 86a, 86b.

National Building Record: 10a, 17a.

The Osterfield Collection (now in the County Record Office): 8a, 9a, 12a, 16b, 23b, 33a, 33b, 34a, 34b, 35b, 38b, 39a, 41b, 42b, 44a, 44b, 46b, 48a, 48b, 50b, 51b, 53b, 55b, 61b, 69a, 70b, 75a.

H. Parrott, Esq: 13a, 22b, 24b, 25a, 26b, 35a, 39b, 43b, 55a, 56b, 58a, 58b, 60a, 68a, 73b, 74b, 94a, 95a.

J. M. A. Paterson, Esq: 79a, 87b.

Mrs O. Paterson: 54a.

W. T. Philbey, Esq: 10b, 18b, 81a, 82b, 83b, 84a, 84b.

A. J. Reed, Esq: 32a, 38a, 62b, 68b, 71a, 71b.

Miss M. Sale: 25b, 32b, 37b, 40b, 51a, 54b, 56a, 59b, 91b, 93a.

E. Viney: 5, 7a, 7b, 8b, 14a, 15a, 19b, 20b, 22a, 24a, 27a, 30a, 30b, 43a, 52b, 59a, 60b, 61a, 63b, 64a, 64b, 65a, 66a, 67a, 67b, 72b, 73a, 74a, 75b, 76a, 82a, 85a, 85b, 87a, 88b, 89b, 90b, 93b.

Miss J. Wakefield: 31a, 57a, 69b, 77b.

INDEX

EPILOGUE

A county town still close to country tradition – the High Street, then dominated by houses, sees the chimney-sweeps celebrate May Day in 1886. This rare picture shows the custom in its last days of 'Jack-in-the-Green', associated with May Day since the middle ages, where a man dances in a wicker framework covered with leaves. It signified the victory of spring over winter and of life over death. The coming of compulsory state education in the 1880s was to destroy traditions such as these, just as the building of the old post-office three years later to the right of the picture was to mark a stage in the growth of the town's commercial life.

1586

D1639696